My First Pocket Guide

Delaware

By Carole Marsh

Correlates with Delaware's SSCF Social Studies Curriculum Framework

THE DELAWARE EXPERIENCE

The GALLOPADE GANG

Carole Marsh
Bob Longmeyer
Chad Beard
Cecil Anderson
Steven Saint-Laurent
Jill Sanders
Kathy Zimmer
Terry Briggs
Pat Newman
Billie Walburn
Jackie Clayton
Pam Dufresne
Cranston Davenport
Lisa Stanley
Antoinette Miller
Victoria DeJoy
Al Fortunatti
Shery Kearney

Published by GALLOPADE INTERNATIONAL

www.delawareexperience.com
800-536-2GET • www.gallopade.com

Gallopade is proud to be a member of these educational organizations and associations:

NSSEA

ASCD

SHOPA MEMBER™
School, Home, & Office Products Association

Other Delaware Experience Products

- The Delaware Experience!
- The BIG Delaware Reproducible Activity Book
- The Delaware Coloring Book
- My First Book About Delaware!
- Delaware "Jography": A Fun Run Through Our State
- Delaware Jeopardy!: Answers and Questions About Our State
- The Delaware Experience! Sticker Pack
- The Delaware Experience! Poster/Map
- Discover Delaware CD-ROM
- Delaware "Geo" Bingo Game
- Delaware "Histo" Bingo Game

A Word From the Author... (okay, a few words)...

Hi!

Here's your own handy pocket guide about the great state of Delaware! It really will fit in a pocket–I tested it. And it really will be useful when you want to know a fact you forgot, to bone up for a test, or when your teacher says, "I wonder . . ." and you have the answer–instantly! Wow, I'm impressed!

Get smart, have fun!

Carole Marsh

Delaware Basics explores your state's symbols and their special meanings!

Delaware Geography digs up the what's where in your state!

Delaware History is like traveling through time to some of your state's great moments!

Delaware People introduces you to famous personalities and your next-door neighbors!

Delaware Places shows you where you might enjoy your next family vacation!

Delaware Nature - no preservatives here, just what Mother Nature gave to Delaware!

All the real fun stuff that we just HAD to save for its own section!

Who Named You?

Delaware's official state name is...

Delaware

Word Definition

OFFICIAL: appointed, authorized, or approved by a government or organization

Statehood: December 7, 1787

Delaware was the first state to ratify the United States Constitution.

A Name of Royal Proportions!

State Name Origin

Delaware got its name from the Delaware Bay and River named after Sir Thomas West (Lord de la Warr), Virginia's first governor. Samuel Argall, a sea captain from Virginia, named the bay in 1610 after he was swept off course in a storm and took refuge in the same body of water discovered by Henry Hudson a year earlier!

WHO Are You Calling Names?

The First State

Delaware is not the only name by which our state is recognized. Like many other states, Delaware has some nicknames, official or unofficial!

Small Wonder

Blue Hen State

The Diamond State

State Capital:

DOVER

Established 1777

Capital of Delaware Since 1777

The capital was moved from New Castle to Dover in 1777 to avoid invasion by British troops. Delaware has had two state capitol buildings. The State House in Dover was the capitol from 1792 to 1933. Some government offices are still located there. The current capitol building was completed in 1933. It is called Legislative Hall.

The Old State House in historic Dover is the second-oldest state capitol in continuous use.

Word Definition

CAPITAL: a town or city that is the official seat of government

CAPITOL: the building in which the government officials meet

Who's in Charge Here?

Delaware's GOVERNMENT has three branches:

LEGISLATIVE	EXECUTIVE	JUDICIAL
The legislative branch is called the General Assembly. Two Houses: Senate (21 members) House of Representatives (41 members)	A governor, lieutenant governor, and attorney general	Supreme Court (5 members, a chief justice and four associate judges) Superior Court Court of Chancery

The number of legislators is determined by population, which is counted in the census every ten years; the numbers above are certain to change as Delaware grows and prospers!

State Flag

State Flag

Delaware's current state flag was adopted in 1913. It features a colonial blue background surrounding a buff-colored diamond in which the Delaware coat of arms is placed. The coat of arms depicts a farmer and rifleman flanking a shield that shows the state's agricultural resources.

As you travel throughout Delaware, count the times you see the Delaware flag! Look for it on government vehicles, too!

State Seal

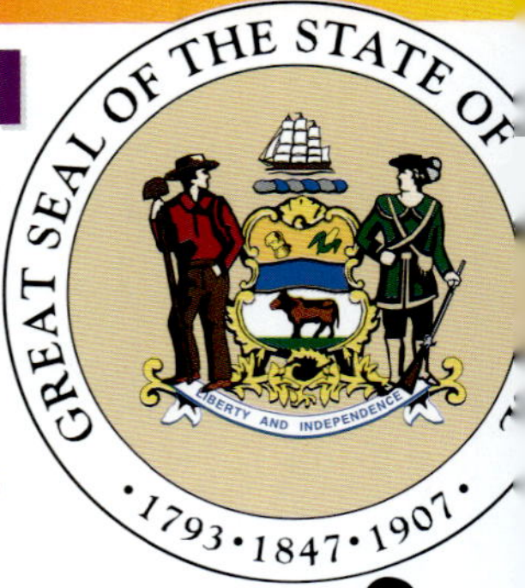

The state seal of Delaware features a wheat sheaf, ship, corn, farmer, militiaman, ox, and water; all represent its role as a farming and industrial state.

Word Definition

MOTTO: a sentence, phrase, or word expressing the spirit or purpose of an organization or group

State Motto

Delaware's state motto is...

Delaware officials adopted the state seal on January 17, 1777. It shows pictures of farming and businesses important to the state.

"Liberty and Independence"

It lies below the state shield featured on the flag. The motto was adopted by state officials in 1847.

Birds of a Feather

The state bird of Delaware is the blue hen chicken. These birds were used to fight other chickens for sport during the Revolutionary War. Blue hen chickens slashed the other birds with their claws and usually won the fight because of their strength. The bravery of Delaware's soldiers during the Revolution earned them the name "the blue hen's chickens."

Blue hen chickens are similar to other chickens. They have blue feathers, no teeth, and sharp bills.

American Holly

State Tree

The American holly grows throughout Delaware. It has dark green, thorny leaves and red berries. Some people create wreaths from its branches and berries during the holiday season.

State Flower

Peach Blossom

Farmers and schoolchildren suggested this as the state flower in 1895!

This blossom is found on the peach tree—*Prunus persica.*

Delaware once grew more than 800,000 peach trees, and was formerly known as the "Peach State." The peach was a big money crop for farmers until 1870 when growing reached its peak. The 1890 peach blight ended the boom and peach production declined steadily after 1900.

RIDDLE:

If the state flower got mixed up with the state bird, what would you have?

ANSWER: A blue peach!

State Butterfly

Tiger Swallowtail

—*Pterous glaucus*

This swallowtail has bright yellow wings tinged in black with blue accents. The larva of the eastern tiger swallowtail feeds mostly on wild cherry and tuliptrees.

State Bug

Ladybug

The state bug is the ladybug. Lawmakers adopted this colorful beetle as its state bug at the request of a second grade class in 1974. Ladybugs are also known as ladybird beetles. They are mostly red, orange, or yellow with black spots. Ladybugs eat aphids, tiny insects that suck the juices from plant leaves.

Like all beetles, ladybugs have six legs and two wings.

State Beverage

Milk

Milk is the state drink. It was chosen because it is healthy, and farmers in Delaware raise dairy cows.

The first dairy cattle in what is now the United States were brought to Jamestown Colony in Virginia in 1611.

Delaware Milk Shake

Take 2 scoops of vanilla ice cream, 1 cup of milk, and blend in a blender with some diced peaches!

Sweet Goldenrod

State Herb

Delaware's state herb is sweet goldenrod—*Solidago odora* It is a *perennial* (which means it lives for more than two years). More than 100 different species of goldenrod can be found in the United States!

Sillimanite

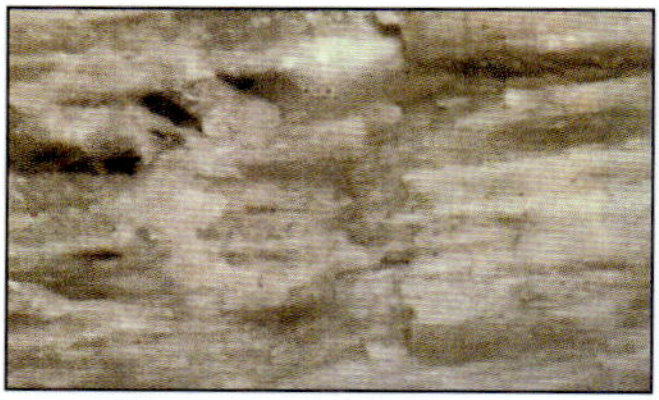

Delaware's state mineral is sillimanite. It is white, brown, and pale green, and found in aluminum-rich rock. Sillimanite has long, slender crystals and is considered an industrial mineral.

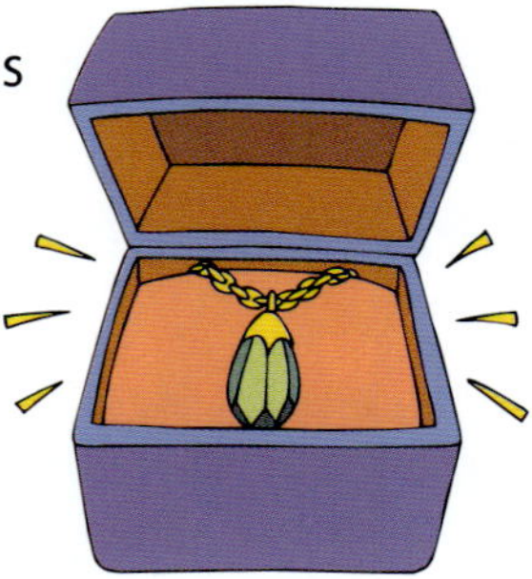

Belemnite

Delaware's state fossil is belemnite

—*Belemnitella americana.*

Belemnites were squid-like creatures that originated in the Jurassic Period, 180 million years ago. Today, these fossils are long and bullet-shaped, with a depression at one end.

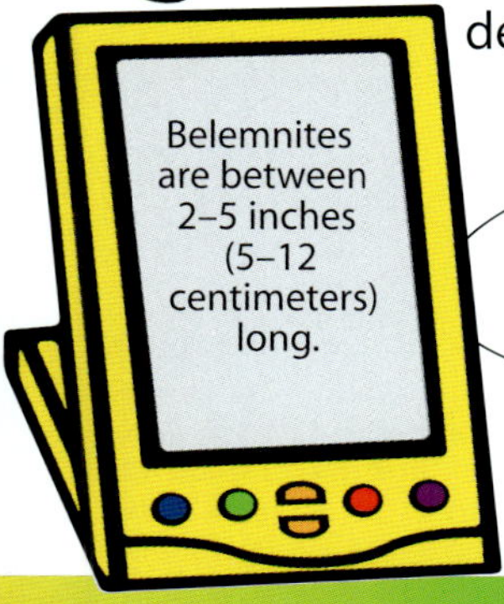

WEAKFISH

State Fish

Delaware's state fish is the weakfish—*Cynoscion regali*. These fish have dark yellow-green or blue bodies and dark spots. Weakfish can grow to be 1–3 feet (.3–.9 meters) long. Fishermen catch weakfish off the coast where they live in shallow water. The weakfish gets its name because its mouth tears when hooked, and fishermen must use nets to scoop them up. Weakfish are also known as sea trout, gray trout, yellow mouth, yellow fin trout, and *squeteague* (skwi-TEEG), which means tiderunner.

TASTY TROUT Recipe

Put a weakfish filet on foil.
Drizzle with lemon juice.
Sprinkle with salt and pepper.
Add shredded smoked ham
and broil fish until done.

The State of Delaware

Delaware is located on America's Eastern Seaboard. Its unusual northern boundary, a semicircle, was part of a circle with a 12-mile (19-kilometer) radius drawn by surveyors in 1701 to mark the portion of Pennsylvania granted to William Penn in 1681. This unusual boundary edges into the southeastern corner of Pennsylvania.

State Location

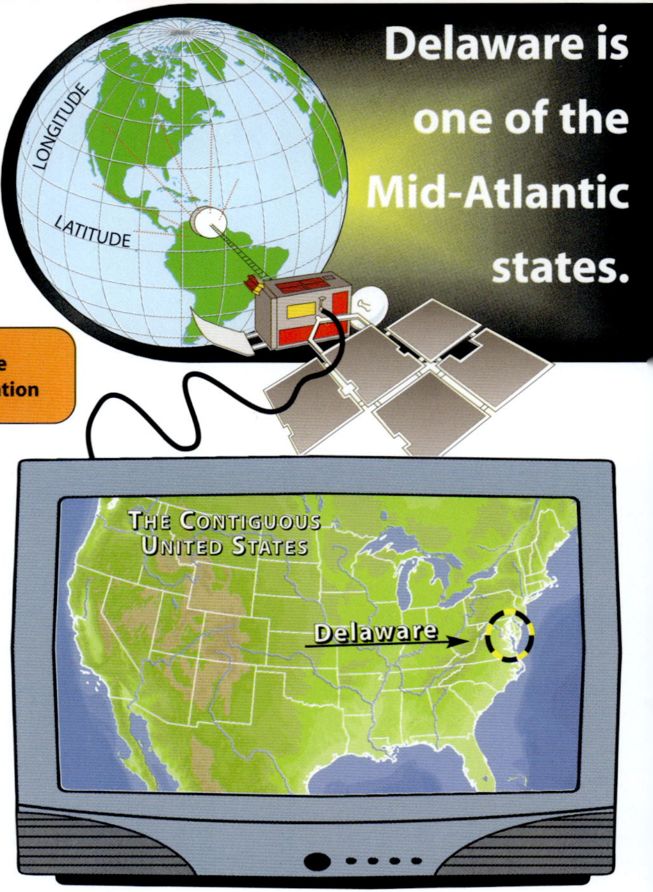

State Location

Word Definition

LATITUDE: imaginary lines which run horizontally east and west around the globe
LONGITUDE: imaginary lines which run vertically north and south around the globe

On The Border!

These border Delaware:

States: Pennsylvania, Maryland

Bodies of water: Delaware River
Atlantic Ocean
Delaware Bay

I'll Take the Low Road...

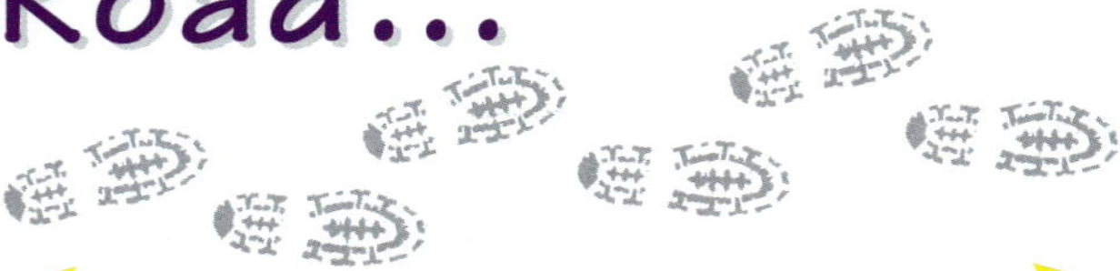

Delaware stretches 96 miles (154 kilometers) from north to south—or south to north. That's a long walk!

Total Area: Approximately 2,044 square miles (5,294 square kilometers)
Land Area: Approximately 1,955 square miles (5,063) square kilometers)

Delaware is 39 miles (63 kilometers) from east to west—or west to east. Either way, it's *still* a long walk!

You Take the High Road!

Highest Point
Ebright Road in New Castle County
442 feet (135 meters)

Most of Delaware lies within the Atlantic Coastal Plain, a flat, low-lying area that seldom peaks above 80 feet (24 meters).

Lowest Point
Sea level along Delaware's coastline

I'm County-ing on You!

Delaware is divided into 3 counties: New Castle in the north, Kent in the center, and Sussex in the south.

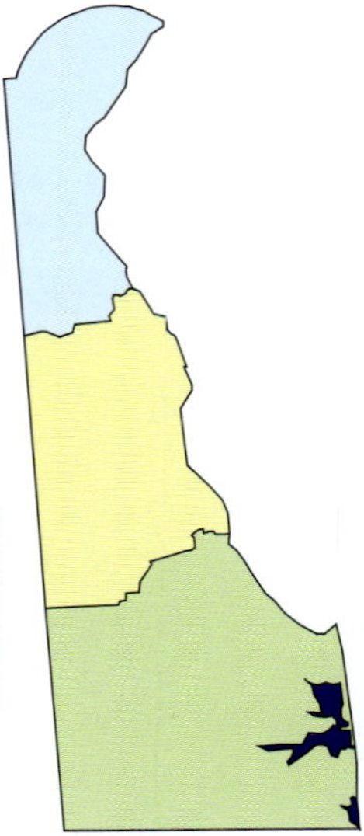

Word Definition

COUNTY: an administrative subdivision of a state or territory

Natural Resources

It's All Natural!

Forests make up about 9,353 acres (3,785 hectares) in Delaware. Forest products are one of the state's natural resources.

Word Definition

NATURAL RESOURCES: things that exist in or are formed by nature

Minerals and rocks:

Delaware's mineral resources are limited. The most widely available commodity is sand and gravel. Minerals and rocks include kaolin, granite, and gemstones.

Weather, Or Not?!

Delaware's temperatures can drop to 35°F (2°C) in the winter and reach 76°F (24°C) in the summer. Its closeness to the Atlantic Ocean provides the state with a very humid climate. Summer can be very hot; winters are usually mild because mountains in Pennsylvania shelter Delaware from harsh northwest winds.

Highest temperature: 110°F (43°C), in Millsboro on July 21, 1930

°F=Degrees Fahrenheit °C=Degrees Celsius

Lowest temperature: –17°F (–27°C), in Millsboro on January 17, 1893

New Castle County receives more snowfall than any other part of the state, about 18 inches per year!

Back On Top

Most of Delaware is flat and low-lying. The Piedmont region features rolling hills and rich valleys. Swampland covers a large southern portion of the state.

Word Definition

TOPOGRAPHY: the detailed mapping of the features of a small area or district

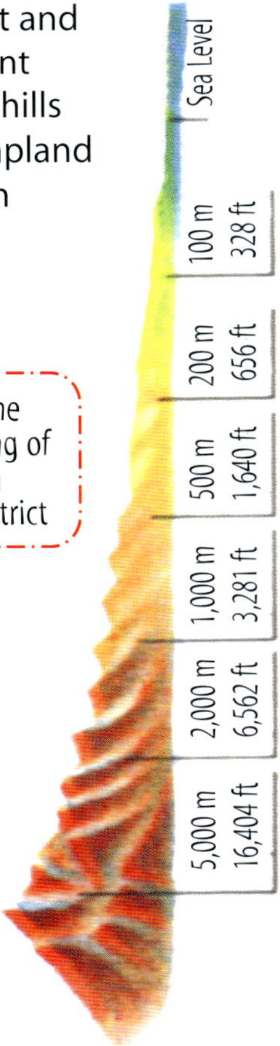

The coastal plain contains many small rivers as well as numerous ponds and marshes.

King of the Hill

Delaware's Piedmont region in the north, features gently rolling hills and scenic fertile valleys. The state's highest point is located here along Ebright Road near the Pennsylvania state line.

Down The River

Here are some of Delaware's major rivers:

- Delaware River
- Nanticoke River
- Chester River
- Choptank River
- Christina River
- Brandywine River
- St. Jones River
- Broadkill River
- Murderkill River
- Mispillion River

The Delaware River gave the state its name and forms part of its eastern boundary.

Gone Fishin'

Delaware has no large lakes. The entire state has only 75 square miles (194 kilometers) of inland water. This area is smaller than some states' largest lakes! But Delaware has a few famous ponds including:

- Lum's Pond
- Killen's Pond
- Noxontown Lake
- Red Mill Pond
- Morris Mill Pond

Delaware has several man made lakes and ponds. Lums Pond covers 200 acres (81 hectares). It also has many fast-running streams.

Word Definition

RESERVOIR: a body of water stored for public use

ARE YOU A CITY MOUSE... OR A COUNTRY MOUSE?

Have you heard of these wonderful Delaware town, city, or crossroad names? Perhaps you can start your own list!

LARGEST CITIES:

- Wilmington
- Newark
- Dover
- Milford
- Seaford
- Smyrna
- Elsmere
- New Castle
- Georgetown
- Middletown

UNIQUE NAMES:

- Bacons
- Hardscrabble
- Gumboro
- Pepperbox
- Rising Sun
- Shaft Ox Corner
- Bear
- Blackbird

Transportation

Major Interstate Highways

I-95

Coleman du Pont Highway
(U.S. 13)

U.S. 301

U.S. 9

Railroads

300 miles (483 kilometers) railroad track, four freight lines, and one passenger line, Amtrak, which services Wilmington

Major Airports

Delaware has two important airports: Greater Wilmington Airport near New Castle and Dover Air Force Base. There is a total of 15 public and private airports.

Seaports

Delaware River

Chesapeake and Delaware Canal

Lewes and Rehoboth Canal

Wilmington Marine Terminal

Intracoastal Waterway

Timeline

- 1609 Henry Hudson discovers Delaware Bay and Delaware River
- 1610 Captain Argall names Bay after Lord de la Warr
- 1631 Dutch settle at Zwaanendael, present day Lewes
- 1638 Swedes settle at Fort Christina
- 1639 Black Anthony, first African, arrives in Delaware
- 1776 Delaware declares independence from Britain
- 1777 Cooch's Bridge, only Revolutionary battle on Delaware soil
- 1781 Dover becomes Delaware's permanent capital
- 1787 Delaware becomes first state to ratify U.S. Constitution
- 1813 Lewes bombarded by British in War of 1812
- 1829 Completion of Chesapeake and Delaware Canal
- 1861 Delaware chooses to remain with Union
- 1865 13th Amendment ends slavery
- 1890 Peach blight ends peach boom
- 1897 Present state constitution adopted
- 1941–45 World War II brings industrial boom
- 1992 James Sills elected first black mayor of Wilmington
- 1998 Banks employ 8 percent of state's non-farm workers

Delaware has a very peaceful history; only one Indian massacre and a small Revolutionary War skirmish reported on its soil.

Here come the humans!

Thousands of years ago, ancient peoples inhabited Delaware. They may have originally come across a frozen bridge of land between Asia and Alaska. If so, they slowly traveled east until some settled in what would one day become the state of Delaware.

Evidence of prehistoric Indians who lived as long as 900 years ago was discovered on the Island Field site near Delaware Bay.

Native Americans Once Ruled!

Delaware's Indians were called the Lenni Lenape, which means "ordinary people." They lived in dome-shaped houses made of bent saplings plastered with mud and cornhusks. The Lenape belonged to the Algonquian family of eastern tribes. The Lenape traveled the streams and rivers in dugout canoes. The women raised corn, squash, and beans. The men hunted and fished. The Lenape traced their descent through their mother's families, and women played an important role in tribal government. Several other Native American tribes lived along Chesapeake Bay, among them, the Nanticoke.

Word Definition

WAMPUM: beads, pierced and strung, used by Indians as money or for ornaments

Land Ho!

Explorers, missionaries, and adventurers came from Europe on ships in the 1600s. The first European to reach Delaware was English navigator Henry Hudson. In 1609, he sailed for the Dutch searching for a waterway across North America to Asia. His ship, the *Half Moon,* sailed into Delaware Bay where he discovered the mouth of the Delaware River. A year later, Samuel Argall, who was from Virginia, an English Colony, was swept off course and found safety in Delaware Bay. He named the bay after Virginia's governor Lord de la Warr. Other Dutch explorers included Cornelius Mey in 1614 and Cornelius Hendricksen in 1616.

A bay is a body of water that extends into the land. Its widest part is at its mouth.

Home, Sweet Home

About three dozen Dutch settlers built a fort and colonized land at the mouth of the Delaware Bay in 1631. They named their town *Zwaanendael,* which means "Valley of the Swans." In 1638, the Swedes colonized a region that is now Wilmington. They called their community *Fort Christina.* England took over the area in 1664 transferring it to William Penn as the southern three counties in 1682.

The Indian massacre of Zwaanendael resulted from the theft of a metal coat of arms from the Dutch settlers by a Lenape brave. The settlers were outraged over the crime. The Lenape chief wanted to smooth things over with the Dutch, so he had the brave put to death. To avenge the death of their friend, a group of Lenapes attacked the Zwaanendael settlement and killed all but one man.

Early Products

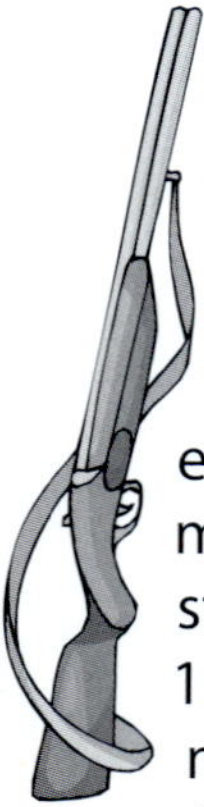

Gunpowder was first manufactured at Eleutherian Mills on Brandywine Creek in 1802. It was the start of the du Pont family's impact on manufacturing in the state which exists today. Farming was most important to the state's economy in the 19th century, with manufacturing inching up in importance. Brandywine Creek provided power for the powder mills, sawmills, and flour mills. Wilmington was noted for its leather goods and fine carriages. Millsboro had its iron furnaces.

Legends and Lore

SOMETHING VERY STRANGE HAPPENED MANY YEARS AGO ON THE DELAWARE RIVER. ACCORDING TO LOCAL LORE, A CARGO SHIP CARRYING PEAS WRECKED ON A SANDBAR, SPILLING THE PEAS INTO THE WATER. THE PEAS SPROUTED, SNAGGING DEBRIS ALONG WITH MORE SAND, AND IN TIME, BUILT UP TO FORM AN ISLAND! GUESS WHAT THIS ISLAND IS CALLED?

PEA PATCH ISLAND!

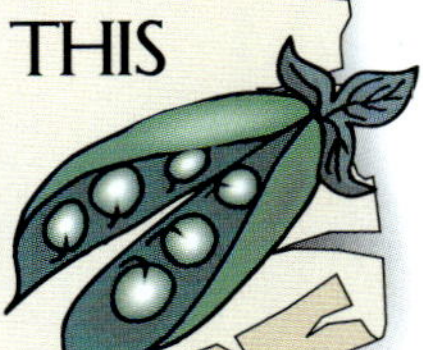

Freedom! Freedom!

Some settlers in the New World felt that England ignored their ideas and concerns. In October 1765, two Delaware delegates, Caesar Rodney of Jones's Neck, and Thomas McKean of New Castle, attended the New York congress to protest the Stamp Act. In 1774, the two men were joined by George Read for the First Continental Congress in Philadelphia. In 1775, the colonies went to war with England. On July 4, 1776, the Declaration of Independence was signed. Kean and Rodney voted for independence but Read was opposed, hoping for peace. Delaware separated from Great Britain in 1776.

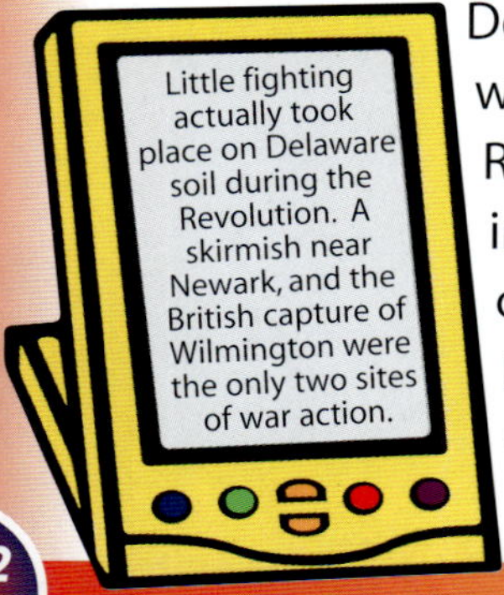

Slaves and Slavery

About 20 percent of Delaware's population was black by 1790; one third of them were free. Delaware was the only slave state where the courts automatically considered a black person to be free unless he could be proved a slave. Although conditions were not as harsh for blacks in Delaware as in other states, they were far from ideal. One of the worst practices was the kidnapping of free blacks to be sold into slavery in the south. In the years leading up to the Civil War, slavery declined in Delaware, but some landowners sympathized with the South. Delaware's people grew divided over the slavery issue. The Underground Railroad, a system which helped slaves escape to freedom, operated a number of "stations" or safe hiding places in Delaware before the Civil War. Nearly 3,000 runaway slaves "traveled" on the Underground Railway through Delaware.

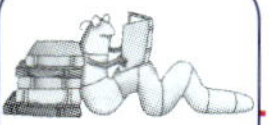

Word Definition

ABOLITIONIST: person who believed slavery was wrong and should be ended

The Civil War

Brother

The Civil War was fought between the American states. The argument was over states' rights to make their own decisions, including whether or not to own slaves. Som of the southern states began to secede (leav the Union. They formed the Confederate States of America. During the Civil War, Delaware remained part of the Union, but hundreds of men fled south to join the Confederate Army. Some people smuggled food and supplies to southern troops. As a result, President Abraham Lincoln suspended the state's constitutional rights during the war. Thousands of men also volunteered to fight as Union soldiers, many losing their lives. The du Pont mills on Brandywine Creek produced more than a third of the gunpowder used by the Union Army.

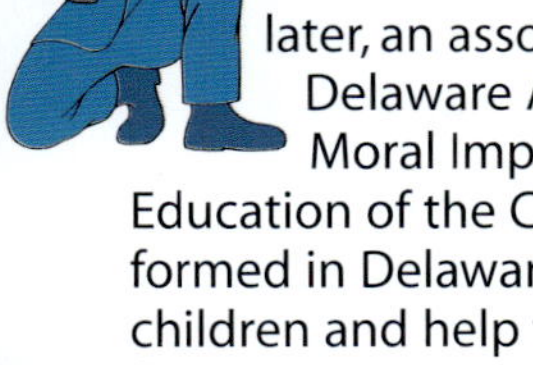

In 1865, the 13th Amendment abolished slavery in the United States. A year later, an association called the Delaware Association for the Moral Improvement and Education of the Colored People was formed in Delaware to educate black children and help former slaves find jobs.

vs. Brother

The Civil War was also called the War Between the States. Soldiers often found themselves fighting against former friends and neighbors, even brother against brother. Those who did survive often went home without an arm, leg, or both, since amputation was the "cure" for most battlefield wounds. More Americans were killed during the Civil War than during World Wars I and II together!

In 1863, the Emancipation Proclamation, freed the slaves still under Confederate control. Some slaves became sharecroppers; others went to Northern states to work in factories.

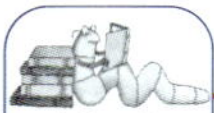

Word Definition

RECONSTRUCTION: the recovery and rebuilding period following the Civil War

Get It In Writing!

1776

—Declaration of Independence

1776

—First Constitution for the "Delaware State"

1787

—U.S. Constitution, Delaware is first state to ratify

1814

—Treaty of Ghent ending War of 1812

1829

—Free School Act passed

Welcome To America!

People have come to Delaware from other states and countries on almost every continent! As time goes by, Delaware's population grows more diverse. This means that people of different races and from different cultures and ethnic backgrounds have moved to Delaware. In the past, many immigrants have come to Delaware from Sweden, the Netherlands, and England. More recently, people have migrated to Delaware from Canada, Italy, Poland, and Hispanic countries such as Mexico. Delaware has many Hispanics from Puerto Rico, a U.S. territory. Only a certain number of immigrants are allowed to move to America each year. Many of these immigrants eventually become U.S. citizens.

1818

Accidental gunpowder explosion at Du Pont claims 44 lives

1890

Another explosion at Du Pont claims 12 lives and destroys 30 Wilmington homes

Disasters & Catastrophes!

1962

Storm pounds Delaware coast for three days, causing seven deaths and $22 million in damages

1967

Riots in Wilmington

Legal Stuff

1897

Present Delaware Constitution is adopted

1920

Delaware refuses to ratify the 19th Amendment which gives women the right to vote; Tennessee's ratification passes the right nationwide

1971

General Assembly passes Coastal Zone Act; state's seacoast is protected from industrial development

1981

General Assembly passes Financial Center Development Act; large number of banks are attracted to Delaware

1884

Emalea Pusey Warner founds Wilmington's Associated Charities

1930s

Cecile Steele introduces the modern poultry industry to Delmarva Peninsula

1952

Shirley Bulah and Ethel Belton, both African-Americans, admitted to all-white schools in their neighborhood

Fight! Fight! Fight!

Wars that impacted Delawareans include:

- French and Indian Wars
- Revolutionary War
- War of 1812
- Mexican-American War
- Civil War
- Spanish-American War
- World War I
- World War II
- Korean War
- Vietnam War
- Persian Gulf War

Delaware! First and Foremost in America's History

Delawareans are proud that their state was the first to ratify the United States Constitution in 1787. In recognition of this historical fact, Delaware is always in first place when all 50 states participate in an event such as a presidential inaugural parade. In recognition, it was also the first state to have its commemorative state quarter minted in 1999.

Indian Tribes

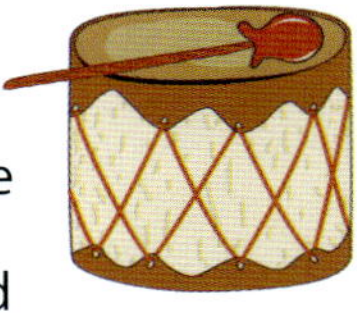

Native Americans have lived in Delaware for at least 10,000 years. The first Indians to greet European explorers were the *Lenni Lenape*. The English called them the *Delaware* because they lived at the bay named after Lord de la Warr. They were mostly peaceful Indians who traded fur pelts with the Europeans for guns, metal, beads, and other goods. Unfortunately, the early visitors also brought along diseases, and a way of life which eventually caused the end of the Lenni Lenape in Delaware. Those who survived moved west.

Zwaanendael, Delaware's first Dutch settlement, was raided by the Lenape in 1632 to avenge the death of one of their braves. Only one settler survived the attack. Around 1690, the Lenape left Delaware.

Diseases introduced by the Europeans, such as small pox, were devastating to the Indian population because they had no natural immunity.

Indians called the *Nanticoke* from Maryland's Eastern Shore, also occupied a portion of Delaware. Despite a smallpox epidemic, the Nanticoke survived the arrival of the white man, but eventually moved to Iroquois country in Pennsylvania and later, west.

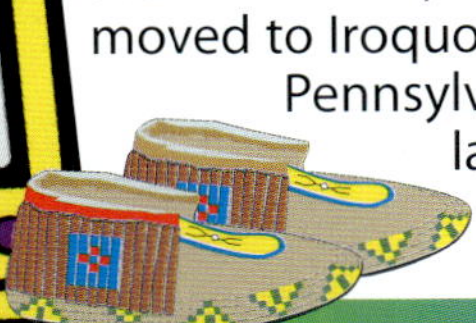

Here, There, Everywhere!

HENRY HUDSON of England discovered Delaware Bay and the Delaware River in 1609.

In 1610, **SAMUEL ARGALL** named the bay and river after Lord de la Warr, governor of the English Colony of Virginia.

The Dutch exploring Delaware included **CORNELIUS MEY** in 1614 and **CORNELIUS HENDRICKSEN** in 1616.

Swedish colonists led by **PETER MINUIT** settled in present day Wilmington in 1638.

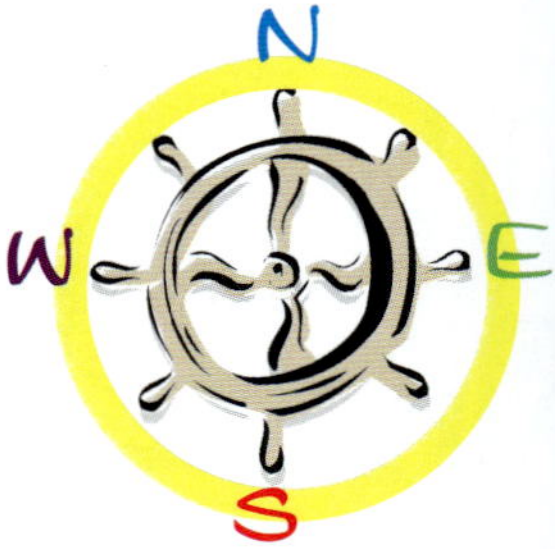

Founding Fathers

THOMAS McKEAN—lawyer, first among Delaware's statesmen to favor American independence from England

GEORGE READ—lawyer who voted against separation from England, later signed the Declaration of Independence

JOHN DICKINSON—"penman of the Revolution," known for his pamphlets against British colonial policies

CAESAR RODNEY—landowner and lawyer; cast tie-breaking vote in Delaware delegation favoring independence from England

COLONEL JOHN HASLET—led the regiment known as the Blue Hen's Chickens in the Revolution

DR. JAMES TILTON—surgeon, abolitionist, and agriculturist; born in colonial era

ELEUTHERE IRENEE DU PONT—began manufacturing gunpowder on Brandywine Creek

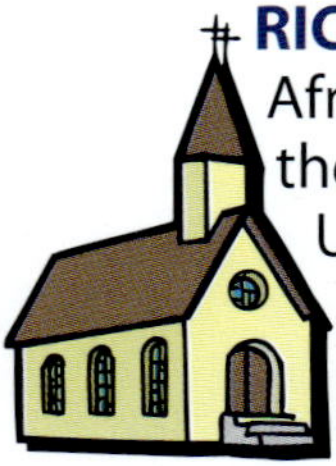

RICHARD ALLEN—founded the African Methodist Episcopal Church, the first black church in the United States

WILLIAM "JUDY" JOHNSON—professional baseball player; helped young black players enter the major leagues

JAMES SILLS—elected first black mayor of Wilmington in 1992

LITTLETON P. MITCHELL—flight instructor for Tuskeegee Airmen; former NAACP president

LOUIS P. REDDING—first African-American attorney

African-Americans make up about 19 percent of Delaware's population, although statewide integration was not achieved until the early 1960s. The summer of 1967 was filled with riots in Wilmington triggered by the economic and employment woes of its black population. The late 1970s and 1980s brought social change and restoration to Delaware's decaying cities through innovative economic and employment programs.

DID SOMEONE SAY BOO!?

Delaware's Governor's Mansion, built in 1790, is haunted by four different ghosts! The first ghost was seen in 1805 by a guest staying at the house who reported seeing a "stranger upstairs." The stranger could be the original owner, Charles Hillyard, who died in the house. Another ghost is a man in a powdered colonial wig who likes to drink wine! The third is reportedly the ghost of a slave kidnapper who "hangs out" around an old poplar tree in the yard. On moonlit nights, he can be spotted dangling from the tree! The fourth ghost is a little girl who turned up at the 1985 inaugural reception of Governor Michael Castle. Many guests complained that an invisible presence was pulling at their clothing!

DO YOU BELIEVE IN GHOSTS?

DELAWARE WIZARDS—soccer team

DELAWARE SMASH—tennis team; former members include Serena Williams and Martina Navratilova

DAYNA PEDEN, New Castle—swam the Delaware River in 1998 at age 11

Sports Stuff

LAURIE MERTON—professional golfer; won 1993 Women's Open

Racing is a big sport for horses and cars! Dover Downs features auto and horse racing. There are racetracks for harness racing in Brandywine and Harrington. Wilmington's Delaware Park provides thoroughbred racing.

Entertainers

GEORGE THOROGOOD—musician and rock and roll artist with the Delaware Destroyers, recorded "Bad to the Bone"

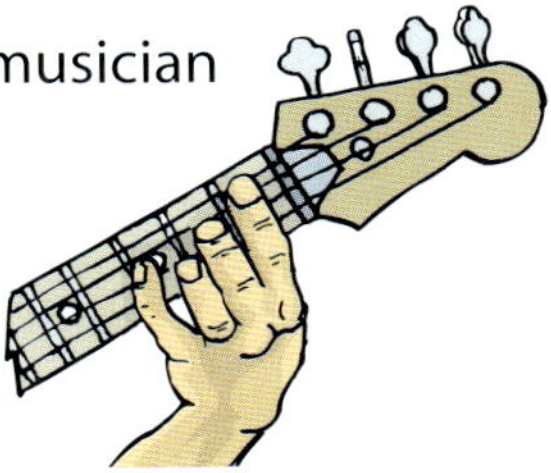

VALERIE BERTINELLI—actress who starred in television sitcoms; continues to work in made-for-TV movies

JOHN BERNARD—actor, producer; headed the state's first theater troupe

JUDGE REINHOLD—film actor; appeared in *Beverly Hills Cop*

Authors

Robert Montgomery Bird—playwright and novelist; wrote *The Gladiator*

John Dickinson—known as the "penman of the Revolution"

John Lofland—wrote poems and stories with Delaware settings

John Phillip Marquand—won the Pulitzer Prize in fiction for *The Late George Apley*

Jay Saunders Redding—wrote about black history and culture in *On Being Negro in America*

Upton Sinclair—wrote *The Jungle;* a Pulitzer Prize winner

Christopher Ward—wrote history-based novels on Delaware

Henry Seidel Canby—journalist, author; founded the *Saturday Review* magazine

Stephen Wallis "Pop" Merihew journalist—wrote *The Quest for the Davis Cup*

Hezekiah Niles—journalist; published *Niles Weekly Register*

George Alfred Townsend—wrote about Civil War; wrote *Tales of the Chesapeake*

Artists

- **Gustavus Hesslius**—Swedish immigrant and Delaware's first portrait painter

- **Henry Lea Tatnall**—19th century landscape painter

- **J.D. Chalfont**—painted scenes of Delawareans at work and play during the 19th century

- **Howard Pyle**—opened art school in Wilmington in 1900 offering classes free of charge to young artists of exceptional talent

- **Joe Moss**—contemporary sculptor noted for large steel works; created sculpture for outside the Delaware Art Museum

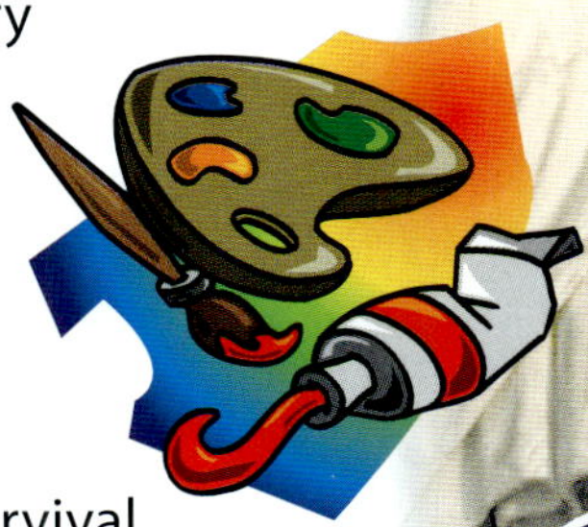

- **Ed Loper**—painter who captures spirit of urban survival

The name du Pont is synonymous with Delaware. E.I. du Pont's immigration to Delaware from France in 1802 marked the beginning of a manufacturing company that will celebrate its bicentennial anniversary in July 2002. Du Pont's original gunpowder plant gave way to the development of synthetic fibers in the 20th century with the production of nylon in 1938. Today, Du Pont is a leader in biotechnology. Their slogan is "The miracles of science." Notable du Ponts include:

Henry Algernon, military officer and politician; *Henry Francis*, horticulturist and founder of the Winterthur Museum and Gardens; *Pierre Samuel*, industrialist and board chairman of Du Pont; and Delaware's patron of education; *Pierre Samuel "Pete" IV* lawyer, politician, and former governor.

WALLACE HUME CAROTHERS—chemist who developed nylon

OLIVER EVANS—invented first high-pressure steam engine and first self-propelled land vehicle

THOMAS GARRETT—abolitionist; helped 3,000 slaves escape through the Underground Railroad

DANIEL NATHANS—shared Nobel prize for research on molecular genetics

S.B. WOO—scientist, politician, former Delaware lieutenant governor

JOHN G. TOWNSEND—entrepreneur, colleague of Pierre du Pont; committed to advancing state's public school system

ANNIE JUMP CANNON—astronomer; called "census taker of the sky;" referenced more than 200,000 stars

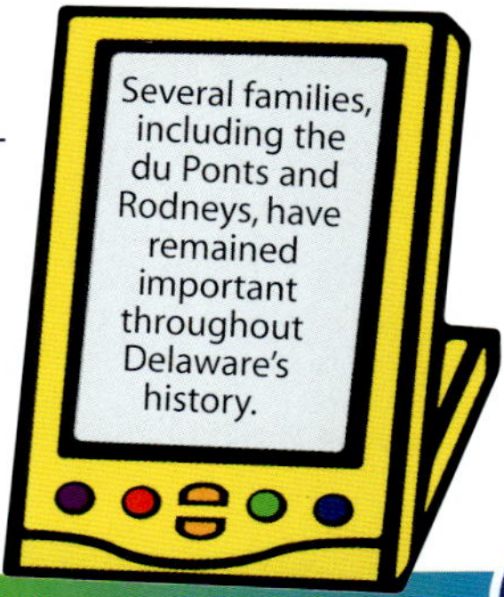

Political Leaders

THOMAS FRANCIS BAYARD—U.S. Senator and U.S. Secretary of State

JOSEPH BIDEN—politician and U.S. Senator

GEORGE GRAY—politician, U.S. Senator, and judge

JOHN WILLIAMS—U.S. Senator

RUTH ANN MINNER—Governor

JOHN C. CARNEY, JR.—Lieutenant Governor

EDWARD J. FREEL—Secretary of State

JANE BRADY—Attorney General

BAD GUY

EDWARD "BLACKBEARD" TEACH—1700s pirate who terrorized the Atlantic Coast; hid his treasure at Blackbird Creek

GOOD GUYS

PATTY CANNON—smuggled free blacks into the south to be sold into slavery

THOMAS COLEMAN DU PONT—Father of the Superhighway, used his own money to build a highway the length of Delaware in 1924

THOMAS KIMBER—a Quaker who formed the Delaware Association for the Moral Improvement and Education of the Colored People in 1866

Churches and Schools

Keeping the Faith

CHURCHES

- St. Anthony's Roman Catholic Church, Wilmington
- Bethel A.M.E. Church, Wilmington
- Immanuel Episcopal Church, New Castle
- Old Swedes Church, Wilmington
- Asbury Methodist Church, Wilmington
- First Presbyterian Church, Wilmington
- Old Drawyer's Church, Odessa
- Christ Episcopal Church, Dover
- Barratt's Chapel, Frederica

SCHOOLS

- University of Delaware, Newark
- Delaware State College, Dover
- Goldey Beacom College, Wilmington
- Wesley College, Dover
- Wilmington College, New Castle
- Brandywine College of Widener University, Wilmington

Old Swedes Church is the oldest church in the United States still in use.

HISTORIC SITES

- **Old Town Hall, Wilmington**—home of the Historical Society of Delaware
- **Willington Square, Wilmington**
- **Pea Patch Island and Fort Delaware**—used as a Civil War prison for captured Confederate soldiers
- **Cooch's Bridge, Newark**—site of the state's only Revolutionary War Battle
- **Old Court House, Dover**—Delaware's colonial capitol

PARKS

- **Bombay Hook National Wildlife Refuge, Dutch Neck Crossroads**
- **Kent and Kelly Islands**
- **The Green, Dover**
- **Delaware Seashore State Park, near Dewey Beach**
- **Trapp Pond State Park, near Whaleys Crossroads**
- **Primehook National Wildlife Refuge, Primehook Beach**
- **Fort Delaware State Park, Delaware City**

Early Residency

- **HALE–BYRNES HOUSE, STANTON**—18th-century house where George Washington held a council of war

- **CORBIT–SHARP HOUSE, ODESSA**—1774 brick mansion with beautiful woodwork

- **WILSON WARNER HOUSE, ODESSA**—1828

- **ALLE HOUSE, SMYRNA**—mid 18th century plantation house still used as residence

- **GEORGE READ II HOUSE AND GARDEN, NEW CASTLE**

- **JOHN DICKINSON PLANTATION, DOVER**

- **FISHER MARTIN HOUSE, LEWES**—1728, moved from Cool Spring

- **OLD DUTCH HOUSE, NEW CASTLE**—late 18th-century

A few of Delaware's famous Forts

- **FORT CHRISTINA**—present-day park near Wilmington where the Swedes built first log cabins in America in 1638
- **FORT CASIMIR**—first Dutch settlement in present-day New Castle
- **FORT DELAWARE**—a mile off Delaware City, on Pea Patch Island, completed in 1859

A famous Delaware Battlefield

- **COOCH'S BRIDGE**—colonial troops held off the British at this site near Newark

Libraries

Check out the following special Delaware libraries! (Do you have a library card? Have you worn it out yet?!)

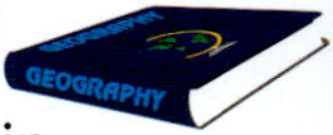

WILMINGTON INSTITUTE FREE LIBRARY—oldest continuous library in the state

UNIVERSITY OF DELAWARE'S MORRIS LIBRARY, NEWARK—has about 1.5 million books, largest library in state

HALL OF RECORDS, DOVER—contains original charter for Delaware Territory

HISTORICAL SOCIETY OF DELAWARE, WILMINGTON—houses many historical state documents

WINTERTHUR MUSEUM, WILMINGTON—books on America and decorative arts

DU PONT AND HERCULES EXPERIMENTAL STATIONS AT WILMINGTON AND NEWARK—large chemical libraries

Zoos and Attractions

NEMOURS MANSION AND GARDENS—a 300-acre (121 hectares) estate with formal French gardens and 102-room Louis XVI-style house built by Alfred I. du Pont in 1910

GREAT SAND HILL NEAR LEWES—100 feet (30 meters) high sand dune; grows taller every year as the ocean pushes more sand upon it

OCTAGONAL SCHOOLHOUSE, DOVER—one of Delaware's first free public schools

BRANDYWINE PARK, WILMINGTON—designed by Frederick Law Olmstead, creator of New York City's Central Park and the National Zoo in Washington, D.C. Home of a zoo, planetarium, and the Josephine Garden

Museums

WINTERTHUR MUSEUM, WILMINGTON—premier museum of American furniture, and decorative arts, formerly the private residence of Henry Francis du Pont

HAGLEY MUSEUM AND ELEUTHERIAN MILLS, WILMINGTON—1802, original gunpowder mills, workers' houses and school on a 230-acre (93 hectares) site

DELAWARE AGRICULTURAL MUSEUM, DOVER—reconstruction of a 19th century Delaware farm

ISLAND FIELD MUSEUM, DOVER—burial ground for about 140 Native Americans

NANTICOKE INDIAN MUSEUM, MILLSBORO

FENWICK ISLAND LIGHTHOUSE, SUSSEX COUNTY—built in 1857

ZWAANENDAEL MUSEUM, LEWES—patterned after a town hall in the Netherlands

AMSTEL HOUSE MUSEUM, NEW CASTLE—contains 18th century household artifacts

CANNONBALL HOUSE AND MARINE MUSEUM, LEWES—has British cannonball lodged in its wall from war of 1812

Lest We Forget

MONUMENTS

DEVRIES MONUMENT, LEWES—erected in 1909 to commemorate the colonists who settled Zwaanendael and were wiped out in an Indian attack in 1632

RODNEY SQUARE—features statue of Caesar Rodney on horseback in recognition of his ride to Philadelphia, July 1, 1776, when he cast the deciding vote for the colony to accept the Declaration of Independence

FORT CHRISTINA MONUMENT, NEAR WILMINGTON marks the first Swedish settlement in Delaware

The Arts

DELAWARE ART MUSEUM, WILMINGTON

GRAND OPERA HOUSE, WILMINGTON—serves as the state's Center for the Performing Arts

THE PLAYHOUSE, WILMINGTON—hosts theatrical productions

BRECK'S MILL ON BRANDYWINE CREEK, WILMINGTON—venue for actors and musicians

VILLAGE OF ARDEN—productions by Shakespeare and Gilbert and Sullivan

SEASHORES

DELAWARE SEASHORE STATE PARK, REHOBOTH BAY

CAPE HENLOPEN, BETWEEN DELAWARE BAY AND THE ATLANTIC OCEAN—site of the Delaware Breakwater, first structure of its kind in the western hemisphere

FENWICK ISLAND LIGHTHOUSE, SUSSEX COUNTY—built in 1857

REHOBOTH BEACH—the Nation's Summer Capital

LET THERE BE LIGHT!

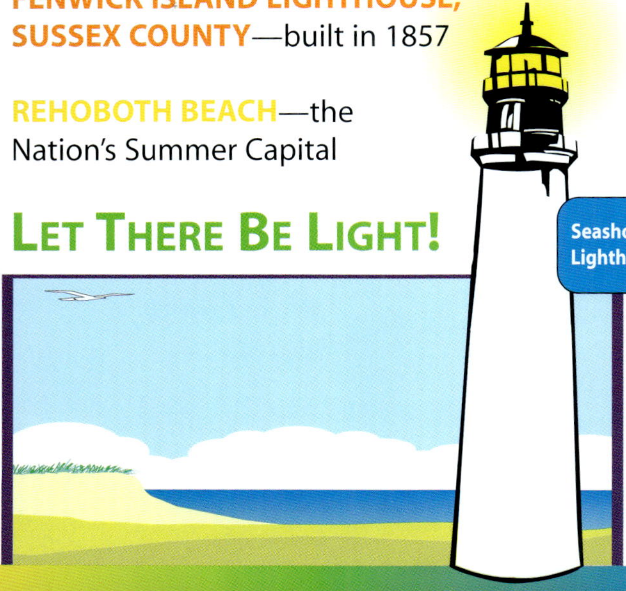

Roads,

COLEMAN DU PONT HIGHWAY (U.S. 13)—runs north-south; length of state; completed in 1924

Bridges,

DELAWARE MEMORIAL BRIDGE—twin spans link industrial area of Wilmington to New Jersey

and More!

CHESAPEAKE AND DELAWARE CANAL—most important artificial waterway in state; forms a link to **INTRACOASTAL WATERWAY**

DELAWARE RIVER—served as a shipping highway for three centuries

Swamps and Marshes

Great Pocomoke Swamp, or Big Cypress, once covered 50,000 acres (20,234 hectares) on Delaware's southern border. In the past, the swamp was the scene of spectacular fires, part of the natural cycle of destruction and renewal. In 1787, the flames of a major blaze could be seen 70 miles or (113 kilometers) away. The last major fire was in 1930. Thousand Acre Marsh is the largest freshwater tidal wetland in northern Delaware. The Chesapeake and Delaware Canals border the marsh.

??QUESTION??

• What is a SWAMP?

Answer: A swamp or marsh is a soggy tract of land formed when a lake is filled in, or water runs slowly over a flat, low-lying area.

Delaware's Animals Include:

DEER
FOXES
BEAVERS

MINKS
OTTERS
RABBITS

MUSKRATS
TURTLES
SNAKES

Beavers dam streams with sticks and mud to form ponds around their big one-room houses with underground entrances.

Some endangered Delaware animals are:

Eastern Puma

Sea Turtle

Sturgeon

Whale

Birds

Blue Herons
Ducks
Hawks
Cardinals
Baltimore Orioles
Hummingbirds
Sandpipers
Snowy Egrets
Grackles
Titmice
Woodpeckers
Teals
Finches
Blue Jays

A hummingbird's wings beat 75 times a second—so fast that you only see a blur! It makes short squeaky sounds, but does not sing.

Birds

Don't let these Delaware bugs bug you!

Field Crickets

Pillbugs

Ladybird Beetles

Grasshoppers

Katydids

Mayflies

Mosquitoes

Spittlebugs

Dragonfly

Mosquito

Butterfly

Praying Mantis

Ladybug

Grasshopper

Water Life

Swimming in Delaware's waters:

Shads
Sturgeon
Rockfish
Porgies
Drumfish
Bass
Pickerels
Bluegills
Yellow Perch
Crappies
Rainbow Trout
Blue Trout
Sea Trout
Menhaden
Carp
Catfish
Weakfish
Oysters
Clams

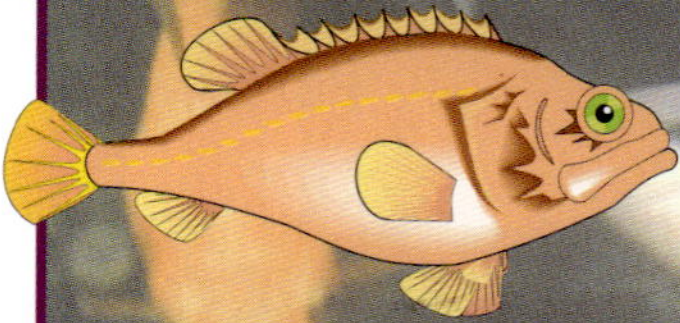

Pond Critters

n Delaware's ponds, you may find:

Hydras
Freshwater Mussels
Pond Snails
Water Fleas
Freshwater Crayfish
Bluegill
Sunfish
Painted Turtles
Eastern Newts
Cricket Frogs
Bull Frogs

You can recognize the cricket toad by the triangle–shaped mark on its head.

Seashells

She sells seashells by the Delaware seashore!

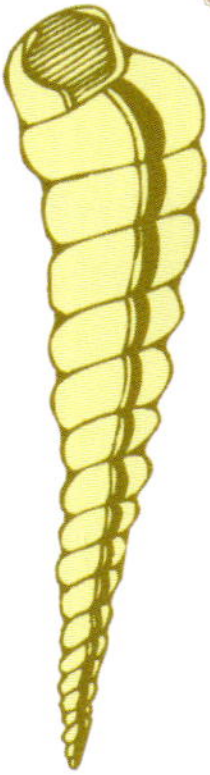

- Channelled Whelk
- Knobbed Whelk
- Periwinkle
- Shark Eye
- Atlantic Slippershell
- Blue Mussell
- Angel Wing
- Blood Ark
- Northern Moonsnail

Delaware has 28 miles (45 kilometers) of coastline along the Atlantic Ocean, a great place to collect shells!

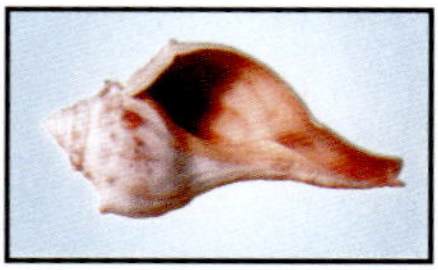
Channelled Whelk

Treemendous!

These trees tower over Delaware:

American Hollies
Hickories
Beeches
Black Tupelos
Pines
Oaks
Sassafrases
Wild Dogwoods
Sweet Gums
Cypresses
White Cedars
Beach Plums
Maples
Sycamores
Walnuts
Laurels
Wild Cherries

Wildflowers

Crocuses
Violets
Butter-and-Eggs
Honeysuckles
Trumpet Vines
Turk's Cap Lilies
Lady's Slippers
Morning Glories
Butterfly Weeds
Water Lilies
Buttonbushes
Ferns
Club Mosses
Egyptian Lotuses
Orchids
Swamp Magnolias
Hibiscuses
Blueberries
Cranberries
Azaleas

Cream of the Crops

Agricultural products from Delaware:

POULTRY

CATTLE

FRUIT

DAIRY PRODUCTS

CORN

VEGETABLES

WHEAT

SOYBEANS

HOGS

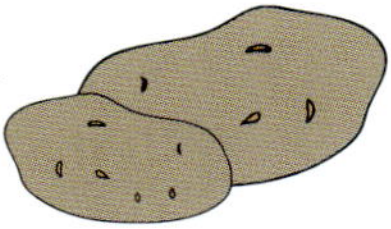

POTATOES

SHELLFISH

First/Big/Small/Etc.

The **biggest sand dune** between Cape Hatteras, North Carolina, and Cape Cod, Massachusetts, towers 100 feet (30 meters) high on Cape Henlopen.

Delaware was the **first state to ratify the U.S. Constitution**, and is the second smallest state in the union.

Delaware is the **only state to have a boundary formed** by the arc of a perfect circle.

Jello was first made in Delaware.

Barratt's Chapel is the **oldest surviving church** built by and for Methodists in 1780 in the U.S.

Nylon was invented in Du Pont's Seaford Plant.

Festivals

Celebrate!!!

Delaware Decoy Festival and Carving Championship, Odessa

Candlelight Tour of Historic Homes, New Castle

Great Delaware Kite Festival, Cape Henlopen

Nanticoke Indian Powwow, Millsboro

Delmarva Chicken Festival, Delmarva

Punkin' Chunkin' Contest, Lewes

Annual Hispanic Festival and Puerto Rican Day Parade, West Wilmington

Holidays

Calendar

Martin Luther King, Jr. Day, *3rd Monday in January*	Groundhog Day *February 2*	Presidents' Day, *3rd Monday in February*
Memorial Day, *last Monday in May*	Independence Day, *July 4*	Labor Day, *1st Monday in September*
Columbus Day *2nd Monday in October*	Veterans Day, *November 11*	Thanksgiving, *4th Thursday in November*

Christmas, Chanukah, Kwanzaa, Vietnamese Tet, and Chinese New Year are all special celebrations in Delaware.

Famous Food

Delaware is famous for...

the following foods!

- –Fabulous fish caught offshore
- –Tasty clawed blue crabs harvested from Delaware Bay
- –Grotto Pizza, statewide chain founded in 1960, Rehoboth Beach
- –Broiler chickens, largest chicken fry in Delmarva where the meat is cooked in a 10 foot (3 meter) frying pan
- –Scrapple, a cornmeal mush mixed with pork bits, seasoned and sliced for frying

Business & Trade

DELAWARE WORKS!

Delaware has a diverse economy with several major industries. About one third of the state's 200,000 workers are employed in manufacturing, with Wilmington known as the "chemical capital." Other industries include automobile assembly plants, paper plants, textile mills, tanneries, and shipbuilding. The broiler chicken is the major product of Delaware's farmers. Truck crops, (vegetables and fruits transported easily and quickly to city markets, or canning or freezing plants), contribute to the state's agricultural economy.

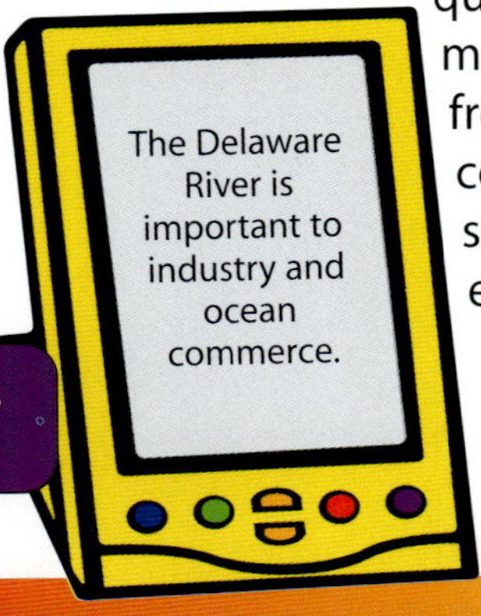

Delaware Books & Websites

My First Book About Delaware by Carole Marsh
America the Beautiful: Delaware by Deborah Kent
Kids Learn America
by Patricia Gordon and Reed C. Snow
Let's Discover the States:
Delaware by the Aylesworths
The Delaware Experience Series by Carole Marsh
Delaware Facts and Symbols by Elaine Kule

Delaware Glossary

GLOSSARY WORDS

abolitionist: person opposed to slavery
bay: body of water that juts into a coastline to form a hollow curve
canal: a channel dug and filled with water to allow ships to cross a stretch of land
colony: a region controlled by a distant country
constitution: a document outlining the role of a government
dune: a rounded hill or ridge of sand that has been heaped up by the wind
emancipation: to be set free
ferry: a boat used to cross a body of water
fort: a building with strong walls for defending against an enemy
immigrant: a person who comes to a new country to live
plantation: a large estate usually in warm climate, where crops are grown by workers who live on the estate
resources: a supply of something that takes care of a need

Delaware Spelling Bee

Here are some special Delaware-related words to learn! To take the Spelling Bee, have someone call out the words and you spell them aloud or write them on a piece of paper.

Spelling Words

paper
abolitionist
agriculture
beaches
Blackbeard
canneries
chemicals
Chesapeake
confederate
ladybug
Lewes
museums
Newark
nylon
Odessa
pirates
shellfish
Smyrna
steeplechase
transportation
Zwaanendael

ABOUT THE AUTHOR...

CAROLE MARSH has been writing about Delaware for more than 20 years. She is the author of the popular *Delaware State Stuff Series* for young readers and creator along with her son, Michael Marsh, of *Delaware Facts and Factivities,* a CD-ROM widely used in Delaware schools. The author of more than 100 Delaware books and other supplementary educational materials on the state, Marsh is currently working on a new collection of Delaware materials for young people. Marsh correlates her Delaware materials to the Delaware learning standards. Many of her books and other materials have been inspired by or requested by Delaware teachers and librarians.

EDITORIAL ASSISTANT:

Pat Newman

ARTISTS:

Kathy Zimmer